Heart2World Publishing

heart2worldpublishing.org

Copyright © 2024 by Oyindamola Shoola

Cover and Illustrations by Morenike Olusanya

ALL RIGHTS RESERVED

No part of this book may be reproduced in any form or by any means, electronic or mechanical, including photocopying, recording, or by any information storage and retrieval system without permission in writing from the publisher and the author.

DISCLAIMER

All characters in this work are purely fictional. Any resemblance to real persons, living or dead, is entirely coincidental.

ISBN: 979-8-3304-5184-5

Printed in the United States of America

FACE ME I FACE YOU

BY

OYINDAMOLA

"Humor can get in under the door while seriousness is still fumbling at the handle."

- Gilbert K. Chesterton -

FOREWORD

In my first year at a Nigerian University, I lived in one of the low-cost multiple-occupancy buildings that serve as the backdrop for this book – usually comprising a shared hallway dividing opposite rows of rooms and communal facilities.

There is a distinct feature of these living arrangements: the elusiveness of a commodity called privacy, creating an abundant market for the commodity called drama – unraveling daily from the intertwined personal lives and identities of occupants with diverse motivations.

'Face Me I Face You' taps heavily into this abundance and more – a reminder of how our social identities and character are shaped (not by the grand gestures and carefully planned outcomes, but) by the cumulative of our mundane interactions with others.

What's also striking is the refreshing simplicity and engaging clarity of the delivery – an efficient thoroughfare to readers, like a hot knife slicing a bar of butter. In 'Face Me I Face You,'

Oyindamola serves an acerbic cocktail of witty humor and unpretentiously clear poems that'll make purists froth at the mouth, but who cares? The audience for this book will love it, even the ones who don't like poetry.

Tolu Akinyemi (Poetolu)
Chief Editor, Poetry Journal
Author, Funny Men Cannot be Trusted

Contents

Palava **12**
How I Got This Ring 15
A Visitor From Hell 17
Iya Ijo 19
Baba Sade's Jalopy 21
Efo Riro 23
A Shelf Of Voices 24
Father 25
The Things Time Tells 26
A Naija Christmas 27
Face Me I Face You **28**
Madam Koi Koi 31
Delilah Took My Breath Away 32
A Name For Their Kind 33
Broda Samson 35
Good Husband Material 37
We Have Never Seen God 38
New Year, New Me 39
A Head For A Cap 40
Enemies Of Progress 41
Water & Garri **42**
Love At First Account 44

Love Doesn't Cost A Dime 45

Hold Me Close 46

Breakfast 47

Dancing Reggae To My Blues 48

How Do You Like Your Poetry? 49

Omo Ibadan Kini So? 50

The Interview 51

Chicken Peri Peri 52

You'll Know It Is Love 53

One More Minute 54

I Asked Maami Where Time Went 55

Assurance 56

Breaking Up With The Moon 57

About The Author 59

Books By Oyindamola 59

Acknowledgements 60

Giving Back 61

Blurbs 62

About The Book 64

Face Me I Face You Playlist 64

PALAVA

Fela Kuti, the pioneer of Afrobeat, used *Palava* as a refrain for his 1972 classic tune *Trouble Sleep Yanga Wake Am*. The Nigerian slang, a pidgin derivative of the English word 'Palaver,' means trouble.

Palava explores the family dynamics across two generations from the perspective of an unnamed character who witnesses the unfolding drama.

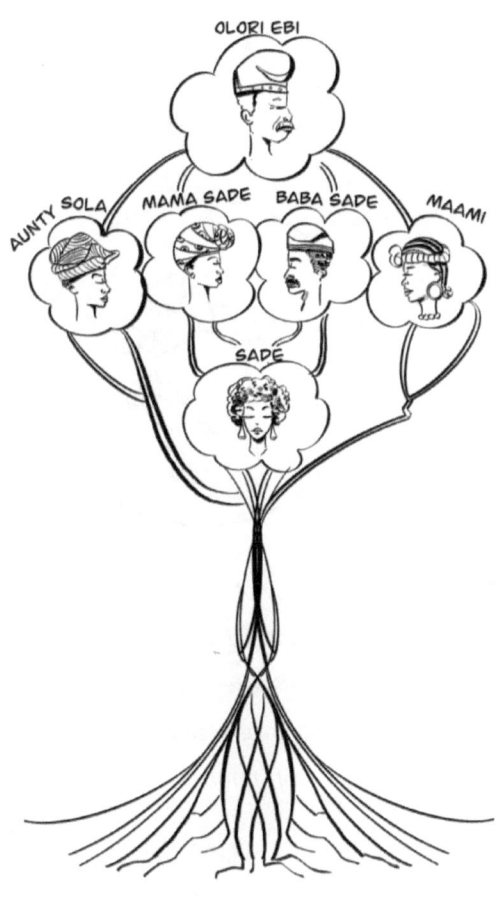

Maami, *the youngest of Olori Ebi's children, is often underestimated due to her gentle demeanor. Her raised eyebrow and side-eye reveal a different nature that catches people off-guard.*

How I Got This Ring

Across the door
Maami stared in horror
with her arms folded
and tongue loaded.

I, almost kissing thirty
as single as a digit
a tenant in Maami's house
clothed in her stolen blouse
twerked to Cardi B's lyrics
as I scrubbed the bathroom sink.
I don't cook
I don't clean
but let me tell you
how I got this ring...

Aunty Sola *is a busybody divorcee who minds everyone's affairs but hers.*

A Visitor from Hell

On Saturday, Aunty Sola visited.
From noon to dusk, she talked
about Lagbaja's marriage to Tamedu
and we knew where this would lead to.

As she gathered her belongings,
ready to leave, she turned to me and said,
When will you find a man to marry
and bring children home for us to carry?

If hell needs fire to rent,
it would be from Maami's sweet mouth
as she replied, *Sola, when your husband returns,*
the one your loudmouth drove insane.

Lagbaja and Tamedu are names that mean anybody and nobody. It is a way of saying so and so.

*Wife to Baba Sade and a fervent prayer warrior, **Mama Sade** possesses a powerful voice that God could gently blow through her speaker-throat to announce Jesus' second coming.*

Iya Ijo

It comes blasting in our ears
louder than the megaphone
of a street preacher
and worse than
the speakers
of a church.

Mama Sade's voice
keeps us up all night.
Waving her brass bell
and a brick-sized bible
she summons God at 3 am
tramples the village witches at 4 am
sings *God of Elijah send down fire* at 5 am
then speaks in tongues to confuse her enemies.
Her speakers take over at 6 am
BLASTING MUSIC
we can't twerk to.

Stricken with insomnia, I wonder
if the God she swears isn't deaf
needs all that noise to hear her prayers.

Baba Sade *is notorious for his discreet adventures around town searching for fresh fish.*

Baba Sade's Jalopy

Baba Sade rode his jalopy around town
from east to west, his eyes wandered,
searching for a 'fresh fish' to hook up.

He found his doom last night
as he drove past Yaba market.
When his eyes landed on a target,
he rolled down his window and shouted,
Fine baby, where you dey go?

It took two blinks to see
his life flash before his eyes.
Mama Sade, whom he left at home,
appeared from nowhere and yelled,
Baba Sade na so you dey do?

Sade *mirrors her mother's spiritual devoutness but masks her true nature in a desperate quest for love.*

Efo Riro

Ever since Sade found a man,
she has not let peace reign in town.
My boyfriend, this... My boyfriend, that...
has made her cheeks fat with delight.

John, the latest boo
Sade tricked with her woo,
lives a thousand miles away
but visits every Saturday.

Sade thinks he visits to see her face
or misplace his hand under her lace,
or cuddle her clenched waist,
or stare at her barrel chest.

But John and I truly know
he is only here for the Efo Riro
that I cook on Saturdays
a thousand miles away.

A Shelf of Voices

Sade, we all know you did not gain
the soprano you used to sway John
from choir rehearsals.

You, who can only boil water
with a microwave, claim to be a chef;
say you've traveled from Spain
to Jamaica, Paris, and London;
read books by Jane Eyre
and written poetry like Shakespeare.

When John bursts into laughter,
a fool for love like you can't decipher
if he is falling deep or calling your bluff.

But if we talk, you'll change to baritone to say,
Jealousy, this is why you don't have a boo.

Father

MY FATHER!!!
Make me your Bureau de Change!
Sade shouted at the altar,
praying after the service.

FATHER! Maldives will look good on my skin,
and let my melanin pop like Otedola's pikin.
FATHER! Relocate me to Canada,
and let my backyard be America.
FATHER! Rolls-Royce is my inheritance,
and let my enemies tremble at my presence!

As I knelt to say a word of prayer,
Sade screamed,
JEHOVAH-ROHI, MY GOD!
Let all my enemies die by fire!

Dreading my sinful thoughts,
I wondered when God became a salesman,
immigration officer, or a hired assassin.

The Things Time Tells

When you disappeared for two weeks
and didn't serve the gram your man's pictures,
we knew you too had been served breakfast.

When you erased your Facebook
and started twerking on TikTok
with your Grand Canyon backside,
preaching, *Buy this bum bum lotion!*
We bought your products
and kept our mouths shut.
#Supportingwomeninbusiness

Sade, we've not seen you in 9 months,
but send you good wishes
as you return with our Lord, Jesus.

A Naija Christmas

What is Christmas if your feet
are not measured with
a broomstick for your mom to find a fit?

What is Christmas
if the bang of local fireworks
hasn't cured your sleepy eyes?

What is Christmas
but death-sentenced chickens
and the aroma of long-throat party Jollof rice?

What is Christmas
without a tailor of undone dresses
stitched with promises and lies?

What is Christmas
without the noise of unavoidable aunties
saying, *I remember when you were kids.*
Or teasing, *When will you marry and give me kids?*

FACE ME I FACE YOU

Face Me I Face You is a low-rent communal housing popular in urban centers in Nigeria. Typically, rooms open into a shared corridor that runs from an entrance to amenities in the back.

This section presents the interconnection of neighbors and their lives through the perspective of the unnamed narrator from *Palava,* who moves out of her mother's house into a Face Me I Face You.

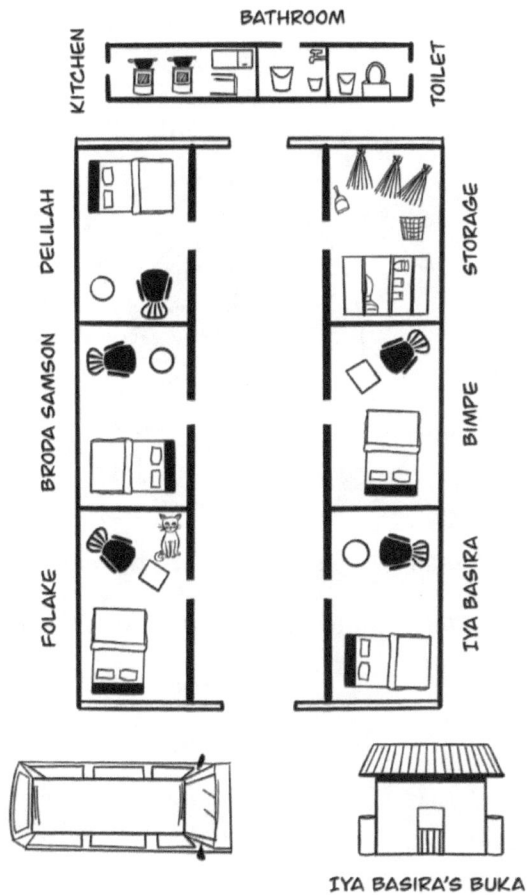

Delilah *is a fashionista and sex worker. She epitomizes the phrase, actions speak louder than words.*

Madam Koi Koi

There are hens whose buttocks
and feathered wings
are exposed by the wandering breeze,
and there is Delilah,
whose skirt will never be long enough
to cover her black yansh.
It is designer, she says,
matching her expensive madness
with a ripped Ye blouse.

There are birds of the air and lilies
of the field whose nakedness
does not castrate our eyes,
and there is Delilah, who
gives the devil thread to
craft a clothless gown that runs
between the crack of her yansh.
I must dress to kill, she says,
as she matches her royal madness
with Madam Koi Koi's red bottoms.

Yansh is a Nigerian Pidgin English term that means buttocks.
Madam Koi Koi is a legendary ghost famous for haunting school dormitories and particularly known for her red heels.

Delilah Took My Breath Away

Today, like a stray,
I paced the hallway,
longing for when she'd pass,
telling my cat, *No one compares.*

When I smelled Delilah's perfume,
I ran out of my room.
Smiling like a tickled child,
I hurried to her side,
but as she talked, my lungs ached.

It used to be her Gucci fragrance
that announced her presence,
but her mouth smelled like decay
and took my breath away.

A Name for Their Kind

What would you call Delilah,
who makes the Garri seller
at Yaba market her first target,
dipping a fist to taste
not once or twice,
then says with a stern face
when asked to pay for her theft,
It is not even that sweet!

        What do you call BroDa SaMson,
        who leaves his apartment and whistles
        at Delilah walking down the street
        but when she turns him down, shouts,
        You're not even that fine!

BroDa SaMson *wears his religion on his sleeves but fails to conceal his extracurricular activities as his path crosses with Delilah's.*

BroDa SaMson

At every service
BroDa SaMson prays
that God will fight his battles
with the same mouth
he tells Delilah at night,
Spread me like butter on your hot Agege bread,
and serve my dinner with your holy water.

At 8 am today, before starting his Honda,
he anointed his bald head
with a shackle-breaking oil
Woli Agba sold for ₦2,000.

Tonight, he'll give Delilah handcuffs
to Kirikiri prison and through the thin
walls, we'll hear him scream, *JESU!*
as she hangs him upside down.

Bimpe *is a single-pringle introvert who desires to marry a wealthy man. Her slogan is 666 – 6 packs, 6 figures income, and 6 feet tall. Any man short of those qualities should not even breathe near her.*

Good Husband Material

Bimpe, you retort when we say A.
>*Men must pay*
>*for the time God spent creating me.*

Yet, you work 21 hours per week
and 1,092 hours yearly, enhancing
the work your perfect God has done.

Before we say B,
you've eyed BroDa SaMson,
screaming with your stiletto throat,
>*I don't speak to*
>*ugly, short, and broke-ass men.*

If we say C,
you will disagree and rant,
>*What's a good husband material without*
>*a Canadian passport, British accent,*
>*and an American bank account?*

We Have Never Seen God

but we have seen the majesty of a cloud,
the gaze of a seducing moon,
stars winking like eyes in the sky,
and heaven teasing closeness, although far.

Bimpe, we have never seen your man,
but we know he wears a gold wristwatch
with a time setting for England,
long beard and a bald head.

Again, on your status this Friday,
you'll teasingly share two glasses of wine
and plates ready to dine.

His face, blocked by your ringless finger,
mocking our curious linger,
by a tickling woo,
Table for two with my boo.

New Year, New Me

Whose lie is worse
between Pinocchio and Delilah,
who claimed *New year, new me* at Shiloh?
Or the tailor who swore dresses
would be ready in time for Christmas…

> And there is Bimpe, saying in January,
> she will start her fit-fam journey
> again. But her body will snitch
> on her tentative truth
> as it is the same story
> we will hear next year.

A Head for a Cap

Anyone who borrows a
flower from Bimpe
without a farm to return,

or an egg without
a flock of chickens to trade,
or a drop of water

without an ocean
in their name, is better off
collecting a cap

from the devil and
giving their head in exchange.
For a Maggi cube

Delilah borrowed,
Bimpe has asked her to use
a teaspoon to fill

the neighborhood's well,
pluck a lioness' whiskers,
and catch a bat's wings.

Sometimes, I wonder
what would become of Bimpe
if she were God.

Enemies of Progress

For two years, you've huffed and puffed.
Yesterday, you did a negativity diet;
today, your cure is a sunbath.
Tomorrow, it will be a gummy bear
the Kardashians share,
and next week, it will be a slimming tea
promoted by an Instagram herbalist.

Even your madness knows no God
and your salvation is on a diet.
When the usher served communion,
you asked for sugar-free wine
and gluten-free bread,
but on your way home
bought Iya Basira's beans and fried yam.

Bimpe, if we talk now, you'll call us *Haturzs*
and say, *I am supporting small businesses.*

Iya Basira's character references a song released by the music group - Style Plus in 2006.

WATER & GARRI

Garri is a popular West African food made from cassava that is processed into a dry, granular form that can be eaten in various ways. To "drink garri" means to mix the dry granules with cold water (and sometimes add sugar, milk, or groundnuts) for a quick and affordable meal. Water and Garri have a similar relationship as peanut butter and jelly.

This section is about the romantic bond between the soon-identified narrator and her lover.

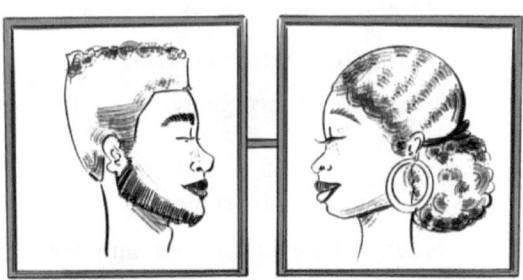

Love at First Account

Recalling their love at first sight,
other people describe
their lover's face, body, or smile.

Folake, all I remember
is when I asked for your number
and you said *Bank account or phone number?*

And we became inseparable since then.

Love Doesn't Cost a Dime

but where I come from
a man who can't climb
the Hyperion to draw
palm wine from heaven
and dig the earth for tubers of yam
larger than Iya Basira's arms
and hunt for a leopard
with five elephant tusks
and cut Aso Oke
directly from Jesus' cloak
and bring sugar, rice, salt,
Fanta, Pepsi, and Malt,
baskets of fruits and assorted biscuits
from the Queen of England,
pay for Alaga Iduro and the song she sings,
pay for the past, present, and future,
pay for merely existing as a suitor...
Such a man is not ready for love.

Hold Me Close

Folake plays with my desire
like a child toys with fire.
When I call her phone,
she dances to the tune.
When I send a text,
she ignores it,
and when I say *I love you,*
she looks at me like it is untrue.

But when I walk away,
she steals glances at me all day.
When I go on other dates,
she cries that I use them as bait.
Yet, when I sing her name around town,
she wrinkles her nose into a frown.

Folake dey use my love catch cruise;
she won't hold me close or let me loose.

Breakfast

I am a child who had
undiluted love for breakfast.

Love was the sneaky apologies
Maami whispered in
Have you eaten?
Try this dress, tell me if it fits.
And her love was the truest.

So, forgive me when I question your blatant
I love you, professed in random moments
and I don't say anything back.

Or instead of forgiving me, reassure me.
Say you love me a thousand and one times
if I ask a thousand times.

And if I say, *Darling, have you eaten?*
Tell me you love me.

Dancing Reggae to My Blues

Folake, when I said beauty is in the eyes
of the beholder, you smirked,
Abegi, close your eyes.

When I said, I want you to be my wife
so we can do this thing together, forever…
you carried your arms above your big head,
snapped your fingers, and shouted *Tufiakwa.*

But today, after talking business and
calling millions even Dangote doesn't have,
you danced reggae to my blues.
Folake, my love for you is
4789 9304 2203 0006
PIN 1234.

How do you like your poetry?

Another woman will wonder
how you like your favorite meal,
if you like your coffee hot or cold,
and the darkest secrets you hold.
If she dares, she'll find out how you like it
behind closed doors and between the sheets.

Look me in the eye and tell me
how you like your poetry.
Do you like sentences that complete you
or lines that open you up to depths
you're yet to know?
Do you like rhythm? Fast or slow?
Do you like rhymes
that chime your teeth and lips
like when we kiss?
Tell me how...

Omo Ibadan Kini So?

I was tasked to describe the treasures of Ibadan.
At first, memories of Mama Ope's Amala,
served with a jungle of meat and Abula,
sunk in a 555 stainless steel bowl
burnt into my finger-licking soul.

But all I could think of was you, Folake,
and how the strokes of your long eyelashes
can tone Ibadan's brown roofs into sliver
and cleanse its street like Christ did our sins.

Although you wash your tongue
into tasteless accents,
Ibadan clings to the home of your mouth,
and its aroma seduces the atmosphere's whistles
when you call cushion, *Kusine,* and chicken, *Sikin.*

Folake, I was asked to describe Ibadan's beauty
and all I could think of was you.

The Interview

The day I feared finally arrived.
I practiced my greetings and what
to say when they ask how we met.

Five minutes before their arrival, I wore
an apron and ruffled my hair,
sprinkled a little flour
on my wrists and dotted Iya Basira's
catfish stew on my white dress.

I poured the stew into a pot,
turned the gas cooker on low heat,
and stirred it like a true chef.

As they licked their fingers,
from Iya Basira's Jollof
to her assorted dessert, I smiled
and thought, the in-laws are impressed!

Chicken Peri Peri

When men call you honey and sugar
or compare you to the sun,
I swear they don't know you!

You strut past their hisses
and honks with your big yansh,
turning their pretentious
admiration left, right, left.

Folake, all these men don't know
what makes your cheeks blush
and your eyes glow,
like when I call you
my chicken peri peri.

You'll Know it is Love

when he calls while you are lying in bed,
and your legs hang upward without support
until the pin-and-needles torturing your feet
knocks sense in your big head.

It is love when every sentence you say begins
with *My bae said…* Family and neighbors worry
he has your mumu button
and has launched its dangerous missiles.

You'll know it is love or a little madness,
but you'll know it is love.

Mumu Button means a soft spot for love.

One More Minute

Sometimes, I wonder why God gave me
only two ears to listen to you.

The first time I heard you speak,
even time ran out of its tick.
You kept saying, *just one more minute,*
but went on and on.

These days, my ears linger
for the gossip your neighbors say
not to tell another or rant about your 999
dresses and how you can't pick one.

Today, when the preacher said,
The sermon will end in 5 minutes
for the 10th time,
the memory of your voice started pouring.
It left me hungry for one more minute with you.

I asked Maami where time went

and she handed me the feet of a child
running topless around the house
the noise of a toddler's endless
what, where, how, and why,
the silence of a teenager's scorn
and loneliness of an absent father
the rebellion of a youthful discovery
the distance of an unraveling adulthood
and the closeness it has brought a lover
a dance of four uncertain feet
to the music of wedding bliss
and an empty canvas
to paint the rest with you.

Assurance

You asked me to swear
I am not looking elsewhere...
Folake, I have told Delilah that
even if she sets herself on fire
she can never light up my world
like your smile.

I have told Sade no matter how
she gallivants her doctor-sponsored palliatives,
it will never stop my heartbeat the way
your brown eyes and smart mouth do.

With love and you, I am learning that
where there are options, you are my only choice.
And if you are not my choice,
I have no decisions about love.

Breaking Up with the Moon

Before we started
worrying about dresses
that didn't fit us

the purpose of life,
the price of lactose-free milk
at supermarkets

dancing to reggae
and singing the blues with wine
at midnight hours

our uncertainties
about the lovers we found
and those we didn't

unruly aunties
who would not mind their business,
and the next due rent

we were once children
riding through the night, thinking
the moon ran with us.

About the Author

Oyindamola Shoola is an award-winning writer, the Co-founder & CEO of Sprinng, a nonprofit empowering African writers, and the Editor & Programs Director at Poetry Journal, discovering widely relatable 'African stories' from ordinary individual experiences.

You can connect with her on Instagram @OyindamolaShoola, where she shares gossip about characters and occasional rants about her experiences.

Books by Oyindamola

Forget It • But Here You Are • To Bee a Honey • The Silence We Eat • Now, I Want to Remember • Heartbeat

www.shoolaoyin.com

Acknowledgments

Face Me I Face You has been a collective labor of love from the beginning to the end.

I dedicate it to my mother, siblings, lover, and best friends, who brighten my life with their quick wit, dramatic satire, and infectious humor.

Thank you to my thesis advisors and professors at American University, Kyle Dargan and David Keplinger, for your guidance in bringing my playful imagination alive.

To my friends and mentors, Poetolu, Ebukun, Kanyin, Dami, Su'eddie, and Tomi, I appreciate your intensive insights and support.

To Morenike Olusanya, I am grateful for your bustling imagination in bringing these characters alive through detailed illustrations and the beautiful cover.

I am also very grateful for the anticipation of my readers on Saturdays, which kept me accountable.

Giving Back

5% of the proceeds from the sale of this book will be donated to programs dedicated to developing and empowering African writers.

To learn more about how you can support, visit sprinng.org/donate or scan the code below.

Blurbs

'Face Me I Face You' is the ingenious equivalent of affordable social housing in Nigeria, where rental properties require tenants to share essential facilities and, inadvertently, their most intimate spaces. Oyindamola cleverly exploits this reality in short but punchy laugh-out-loud poems that use wit and humor to tell profound stories about her vibrant and memorable characters.

Dami Ajayi
Author of A Woman's Body is Country and Affection & Other Accidents

Sharp, Short, and Sweet! Oyindamola's 'Face Me I Face You' invites the reader into a vivid and sensory narrative poetry experience. With a range of exciting characters, Oyin has created a nostalgic page-turner and an ode to the city of Ibadan.

Tomi Adesina
Writer, The Wait

A wonderfully eclectic addition to Shoola's ever-expanding oeuvre, 'Face Me I Face You' is equal parts humor, heart, and homage. Rooted in a rich cultural parlance and a tapestry of familiar characters, Shoola makes magic of the mundane, presenting a witty, compelling portrait of modern Nigerian urbanity. There is nothing out there quite like it.

Kanyinsola Olorunnisola
Founder, Sprinng

Poetry can sometimes be too challenging to comprehend or too profound to enjoy, but definitely not in Oyindamola Shoola's 'Face Me I Face You.' This witty and beautifully illustrated collection of poems offer a fresh perspective on a family living in a shared housing setup, where neighbors' lives intertwine in unexpected and often humorous ways. The book explores themes of family, tradition, and everyday dramas that most of us will easily recognize. From the bustling streets to intimate domestic moments, this collection celebrates resilience, community, and the indomitable spirit of its characters in a way that will leave most readers smiling.

S. Su'eddie Vershima Agema
Multiple Award-winning Author of Memory and the Call of Waters (Winner, Association of Nigerian Authors Poetry Prize 2022 and Finalist, Nigeria Prize for Literature 2022)

'Face Me I Face You' is a brilliant and outstanding collection that comments on social issues through its unique storytelling, characterization, delicate blend of language, refreshing humor, and satire. Drawing from life and culture, Oyindamola takes readers on an immersive experience that leaves them entertained and desiring more.

Ebukun Gbemisola Ogunyemi
York University

About The Book

Face Me I Face You is a collection of poems existing at the interface of identity, class, and culture. It holds a mirror to the working class by capturing the narrative essence and dramatized aspirations of its characters. The deployed humor fondly humanizes our modern realities and reaches beyond the tragedy of these colorful archetypes of city life.

Face Me I Face You Playlist

The book references many nostalgic songs by African artists that you can enjoy by scanning the codes below or visiting the links.

Spotify: Tinyurl.com/FMIFYSpotify
YouTube: Tinyurl.com/FMIFYYouTube

Spotify Playlist   *YouTube Playlist*

www.ingramcontent.com/pod-product-compliance
Lightning Source LLC
LaVergne TN
LVHW041714060526
838201LV00043B/731